Dear Beautiful Me...

Copyright© 2020 by Veronique L. Pericles

All rights reserved. This book or any portion thereof may not be used in any manner whatsoever without the written permission of the author or publisher except for the brief quotations in a review, in which Author and Publisher shall be notably mentioned. This book may only be reproduced by the Publisher and or Distributors assigned by the Publisher.

Printed in the United States of America
First printing, 2020

ISBN: 978-1-7332371-8-5

SELF-PUBLISHING SERVICES
provided by High Maintenance Publishing & Production, LLC

www.highmaintenance1.com

"Providing Opportunities, Inspiration and Education to Independent Writers."

Author Celeste Celeste
High Maintenance Publishing & Production, CEO

#DearBeautifulMe

Hi!

My name is Veronique. I made this journal to help girls who struggle to see themselves positively. Dear Beautiful Me was created to help every girl realize she is beautiful, powerful and strong, through personal expression and positive affirmations. I hope you can see the beautiful girl God made you to be!

Veronique L. Pericles
xoxo

#DearBeautifulMe

This journal belongs to:

_____

#DearBeautifulMe

Parental/Guardian Agreement

As a parent/guardian, your child needs to know you care and understanding that adolescence is a period of change for the both of you is the first step.

Providing guidance and support will always be a continuous effort that can be demonstrated by staying involved, building communication with a willingness to listen, and most importantly, without judgement.

This does not mean that there are not rules and consequences, however it is important to continue to build a relationship and promote positive choices, knowing that mistakes will be made.

Be present, be consistent, be encouraging and provide an open and safe outlet for communication.

We will begin this journey together with a few promises & expectations.

#DearBeautifulMe

Parental/Guardian Agreement

1. I promise to encourage the practice of writing openly and freely as needed.

2. I promise to provide a safe, nurturing, and open-door policy for discussion without judgement.

3. I promise to communicate from a place of understanding & compassion and not from anger.

4. I promise, going forward, to use these experiences as teaching opportunities with an understanding that we both make mistakes but that the focus is to establish a positive outcome.

5. I promise to do my best at handling moments where it may be difficult for you to express your emotions.

By signing this contract I am holding myself accountable and making the above promises to create and promote your creativity and desire for self-expression. I will do so with an intent to learn as well as to provide guidance and support.

Parent Signature:_____

#DearBeautifulMe

Write down how your day was! Good or bad it is important to express your feelings. You can also list any daily chores or assignments.

MONDAY -

TUESDAY -

WEDNESDAY

THURSDAY

FRIDAY

It's the WEEKEND!
List your plans and goals for next week!

SATURDAY

SUNDAY

Goals for next week:

1. _____
2. _____
3. _____
4. _____
5. _____

> *I am a problem solver; I will find a way.*

List five (5) positive things about yourself

1. _____
2. _____
3. _____
4. _____
5. _____

Express yourself!

What were some of the best things that happened this week? What was the worst thing that happened this week?

_____
_____
_____
_____
_____

 Write down how your day was! Good or bad it is important to express your feelings. You can also list any daily chores or assignments.

MONDAY -

TUESDAY -

WEDNESDAY

THURSDAY

FRIDAY

#DearBeautifulMe

It's the WEEKEND!
List your plans and goals for next week!

SATURDAY

SUNDAY

Goals for next week:

1. _____
2. _____
3. _____
4. _____
5. _____

> *No one can make me feel inferior without my consent.* Eleanor Roosevelt

List five (5) positive things about yourself

1. _____
2. _____
3. _____
4. _____
5. _____

Express yourself!

What were some of the best things that happened this week? What was the worst thing that happened this week?

_____
_____
_____
_____
_____

#DearBeautifulMe

Write down how your day was! Good or bad it is important to express your feelings. You can also list any daily chores or assignments.

MONDAY

TUESDAY

WEDNESDAY

THURSDAY

FRIDAY

#DearBeautifulMe

It's the WEEKEND!
List your plans and goals for next week!

SATURDAY

SUNDAY

Goals for next week:

1. _____
2. _____
3. _____
4. _____
5. _____

> *I will show kindness, even when it seems hard.*

List five (5) positive things about yourself

1. _____
2. _____
3. _____
4. _____
5. _____

Express yourself!

What were some of the best things that happened this week? What was the worst thing that happened this week?

_____
_____
_____
_____
_____

Write down how your day was! Good or bad it is important to express your feelings. You can also list any daily chores or assignments.

MONDAY -

TUESDAY -

WEDNESDAY

THURSDAY

FRIDAY

It's the WEEKEND!

List your plans and goals for next week!

SATURDAY

SUNDAY

Goals for next week:

1. _____
2. _____
3. _____
4. _____
5. _____

> *I am a girl with lots of ideas!*

List five (5) positive things about yourself

1. _____
2. _____
3. _____
4. _____
5. _____

Express yourself!

What were some of the best things that happened this week? What was the worst thing that happened this week?

_____
_____
_____
_____
_____

Write down how your day was! Good or bad it is important to express your feelings. You can also list any daily chores or assignments.

MONDAY

TUESDAY

WEDNESDAY

THURSDAY

FRIDAY

It's the WEEKEND!
List your plans and goals for next week!

SATURDAY

SUNDAY

Goals for next week:

1. _____
2. _____
3. _____
4. _____
5. _____

> *I will speak up, even when my voice cracks.*

List five (5) positive things about yourself

1. _____
2. _____
3. _____
4. _____
5. _____

Express yourself!

What were some of the best things that happened this week? What was the worst thing that happened this week?

_____
_____
_____
_____
_____

Write down how your day was! Good or bad it is important to express your feelings. You can also list any daily chores or assignments.

MONDAY

TUESDAY

#DearBeautifulMe

WEDNESDAY

THURSDAY

FRIDAY

It's the WEEKEND!
List your plans and goals for next week!

SATURDAY

SUNDAY

Goals for next week:

1. _____
2. _____
3. _____
4. _____
5. _____

> *I can accomplish anything I set my mind to.*

List five (5) positive things about yourself

1. _____
2. _____
3. _____
4. _____
5. _____

Express yourself!

What were some of the best things that happened this week? What was the worst thing that happened this week?

_____
_____
_____
_____
_____

 Write down how your day was! Good or bad it is important to express your feelings. You can also list any daily chores or assignments.

MONDAY -

TUESDAY -

WEDNESDAY

THURSDAY

FRIDAY

It's the WEEKEND!

List your plans and goals for next week!

SATURDAY

SUNDAY

Goals for next week:

1. _____
2. _____
3. _____
4. _____
5. _____

> *I am important.*

List five (5) positive things about yourself

1. _____
2. _____
3. _____
4. _____
5. _____

Express yourself!

What were some of the best things that happened this week? What was the worst thing that happened this week?

_____
_____
_____
_____
_____

 Write down how your day was! Good or bad it is important to express your feelings. You can also list any daily chores or assignments.

MONDAY -

TUESDAY -

WEDNESDAY

THURSDAY

FRIDAY

It's the WEEKEND!
List your plans and goals for next week!

SATURDAY

SUNDAY

Goals for next week:

1. _____
2. _____
3. _____
4. _____
5. _____

#DearBeautifulMe

> *I can be proud of myself... even if no one else is.*

List five (5) positive things about yourself

1. _____
2. _____
3. _____
4. _____
5. _____

Express yourself!

What were some of the best things that happened this week? What was the worst thing that happened this week?

_____
_____
_____
_____
_____

Write down how your day was! Good or bad it is important to express your feelings. You can also list any daily chores or assignments.

MONDAY

TUESDAY

WEDNESDAY

THURSDAY

FRIDAY

#DearBeautifulMe

It's the WEEKEND!
List your plans and goals for next week!

SATURDAY

SUNDAY

Goals for next week:

1. _____
2. _____
3. _____
4. _____
5. _____

> *I deserve to be happy, I do not need to be perfect!*

List five (5) positive things about yourself

1. _____
2. _____
3. _____
4. _____
5. _____

Express yourself!

What were some of the best things that happened this week? What was the worst thing that happened this week?

_____
_____
_____
_____
_____

 Write down how your day was! Good or bad it is important to express your feelings. You can also list any daily chores or assignments.

MONDAY -

TUESDAY -

WEDNESDAY

THURSDAY

FRIDAY

#DearBeautifulMe

It's the WEEKEND!
List your plans and goals for next week!

SATURDAY

SUNDAY

Goals for next week:

1. _____
2. _____
3. _____
4. _____
5. _____

> My body is perfect the way it is!

List five (5) positive things about yourself

1. _____
2. _____
3. _____
4. _____
5. _____

Express yourself!

What were some of the best things that happened this week? What was the worst thing that happened this week?

_____
_____
_____
_____
_____

 Write down how your day was! Good or bad it is important to express your feelings. You can also list any daily chores or assignments.

MONDAY -

TUESDAY -

WEDNESDAY

THURSDAY

FRIDAY

It's the WEEKEND!
List your plans and goals for next week!

SATURDAY -

SUNDAY -

Goals for next week:

1. _____
2. _____
3. _____
4. _____
5. _____

> *I am fearless and brave!*

List five (5) positive things about yourself

1. _____
2. _____
3. _____
4. _____
5. _____

Express yourself!

What were some of the best things that happened this week? What was the worst thing that happened this week?

_____
_____
_____
_____
_____

Write down how your day was! Good or bad it is important to express your feelings. You can also list any daily chores or assignments.

MONDAY -

TUESDAY -

WEDNESDAY- -

THURSDAY -

FRIDAY -

It's the WEEKEND!
List your plans and goals for next week!

SATURDAY

SUNDAY

Goals for next week:

1. _____
2. _____
3. _____
4. _____
5. _____

> *No one can take away my happiness.*

List five (5) positive things about yourself

1. _____
2. _____
3. _____
4. _____
5. _____

Express yourself!

What were some of the best things that happened this week? What was the worst thing that happened this week?

_____
_____
_____
_____
_____

#DearBeautifulMe